Coastal Steam Vessels of the British Isles

By

A.E. Bennett and Barry J. Eagles

All illustrations by A. E. Bennett unless otherwise stated.

Dedicated to the memory of the late
JOHN MICHAEL DUNN WARREN
a great steamer enthusiast.

First Published 2001   ISBN 0 946184 91 7

Front cover: Whippingham approaching Ryde Pier on the 1st September 1962
(last day of service).

Back cover: Duchess of Hamilton leaving Wemyss Bay on the 18th August 1970.

Frontispiece: The *Consul* in drydock at Southampton in 1964. Barry J. Eagles

Published By

Waterfront

A Division of Kingfisher Productions

The Dalesmade Centre, Watershed Mill, Settle,

North Yorkshire BD24 9LR

Printed by The Amadeus Press, Cleckheaton, West Yorkshire

Introduction

I was born in Folkestone, and when I was 3½ years old my family moved to Hythe in Kent. Here my interest in railways began, as we visited the Romney, Hythe and Dymchurch Railway on numerous occasions, and I became fascinated by observing Walschaerts valve gear in motion. (I still am!) Steamers were only of superficial interest until we moved to Sandown on the Isle of Wight, for besides the paddlers which plied between Portsmouth and Ryde, there were day trips by Red Funnel steamers to Bournemouth where my grandparents lived. This then was my limited knowledge of steamers, as I was still primarily a railway enthusiast.

A visit to a Gilbert and Sullivan opera was for me a Damascene conversion to 'serious' music, which has remained a chief source of pleasure ever since. This meant that when I started work in Woolwich in 1952, my spare cash had to be spread between railway activities and music, (concert going and the purchase of LPs). My interest in railways grew, but apart from the odd railtour, I was unable to get about much until 1955, when my working hours were considerably improved, and I could depend on having most weekends free.

It was in 1955 that I acquired my first 35mm camera, concentrating entirely on railway photography. Two years later I bought a second camera for colour transparencies. My first steamer slide was of the P.S. *Sandown*, followed by the antediluvian Woolwich ferries. It was a lucky chance being able to photograph P.S. *Whippingham* on her last day in service in 1962. At that period, I was not aware that there were any similar steamers still operating elsewhere. It was not until late 1963, whilst participating on a railtour to Weymouth and Portland, that I spotted a paddle steamer in Weymouth Bay. The following year, I visited both Dorset and the Bristol Channel, and I joined the Paddle Steamer Preservation Society, and the Coastal Cruising Association. In the latter society's magazine, I saw a note urging members, who had not already done so to visit the Clyde to see the P.S. *Jeanie Deans* in her last season. This was my real conversion to the steamer scene and it rapidly took precedence over railways, particularly after the end of steam on the Isle of Wight.

My most enjoyable holiday experiences have been sailing on the pleasure steamers, especially in Scotland. A very memorable cruise was aboard the turbine steamer *Duchess of Hamilton*, as we overtook the *Duchess of Montrose* on the last ever Friday 'race' from Rothesay to Largs. If any reader was aboard the *Duchess of Montrose* on that occasion and photographed our vessel about to pass, I would be most grateful for a copy please! Another unforgettable trip, was aboard the Cunard liner *Queen Mary* from Calais to Southampton during 1967 her last year in service (First class single fare a mere twelve pounds). As she steamed sedately past the Fawley Oil Refinery, all the moored tankers saluted the Old Lady, one by one with three deferential blasts, and each received three stentorian blasts in acknowledgement, a most moving experience.

It only remains for me to express my warm thanks to Barry J. Eagles, an authority on steamers and matters nautical, for the great encouragement and help he has given me not least in providing the technical details and amplifying my brief captions. Also to my publisher Roger Hardingham for his interest in the work of a railway enthusiast not widely known for his steamer photography. My thanks are also due to Ron White of Colour Rail, and to Derek Buttivant, without whose chance remark this album might never have been envisaged.   **A. E. Bennett, Norwich**

The magic of steam. The engine room on *Princess Elizabeth* on 4th August 1964.

I have enjoyed having the privilege of looking at Tony's slides and writing the words to the illustrations in this book. I apologise in advance for the large number of Isle of Man steamers, but for most steamer enthusiasts, they are high in our affections. I would like to thank Bert Moody, Keith Adams and Andy Crespin, for their help with some of the smaller steamers.

Barry J. Eagles, Chandlers Ford

CAMERA DETAILS

My first 35mm camera was an inexpensive Ilford Advocate, its wide angle lens in many cases distorting the extreme edges of the resulting images. In July 1958 I bought a Zeiss Super Ikonta, with its superb 3.5 Tessar lens. With this camera, I obtained far more satisfactory results. I nearly always used Ilford film for black and white work. I continued to use 35mm format for colour transparencies, using mostly Kodachrome film, experiments with other films being unsatisfactory. In 1958 I also purchased a Zeiss Contax, which too had a Tessar lens, for 35mm work. I replaced this camera ten years later with a Kodak Retina. This in turn was replaced by an Olympus OM10. I ceased using black and white film entirely by 1968. I now use Fujichrome for colour slides, and Kodacolor for prints.   **A.E. Bennett**

Above: Ryde was launched on the 23rd April 1937 at the Dumbarton yard of William Denny and Brothers, for the Southern Railway, for the same service as her sister *Sandown* (page 24). *Ryde* was called up like her sister *Sandown*, for minesweeping duties during the Second World War. They were both in Flotilla No. 7, based on the Forth. Released from war service, she returned to the Solent to resume her duties. *Ryde* was withdrawn in 1969. In 1972 she was moved to the River Medina on the Isle of Wight, and became a night club, in the same location as the *Medway Queen* (page 17). *Ryde* is seen approaching Ryde Pier on the 18th August 1968.

Right: Squires was one of four similar ferries built for the famous Woolwich Free Ferry, and was delivered from her builders J. Samuel White in December 1922. An Act of Parliament had been obtained in 1885 for a ferry service across the River Thames at Woolwich. Four years later two paddle vessels the *Duncan* and the *Gordon* (1) commenced the service. The ferry service was so busy that it required another vessel the *Hutton* to be built in 1894. These three vessels soldiered on until the arrival of *Squires* and companions. At the time of her withdrawal in 1962, the ferry service was owned by the London County Council.

Squires is seen crossing the Thames at Woolwich on the 7th January 1961.

TATTERSHALL CASTLE
This paddle steamer and her identical sister the *Wingfield Castle,* (See Page 5) were launched on the 24th September 1934 at the West Hartlepool yard of William Gray & Company Limited. They were built for the London and North Eastern Railway's route across the River Humber from Hull to New Holland and summer excursions to Grimsby. On the 1st January 1948 all railway company ships became part of the Railway Executive. Eleven years later *Tattershall Castle* and her sister were transferred to the Associated Humber Lines Company. Later in her operational career she belonged to Sealink. She was withdrawn in 1972 and is now a restaurant ship on the River Thames at the Embankment.

TECHNICAL DETAILS. Powered by a 3-cylinder triple expansion diagonal steam engine built by the Central Marine Engineering Works of Hartlepool, producing 1,200 horse power. With coal fired boilers giving a speed of 13 knots. Their length is 209 feet 7 inches with a gross registered tonnage of 556. They carried a crew of 10 and 1,200 passengers. Approaching New Holland Pier on the 24th June 1964 in the colours of Associated Humber Lines.

WINGFIELD CASTLE
This ship had an identical career to her sister ship the *Tattershall Castle* (page 4) until she was withdrawn in 1974. She was bought initially for conversion into a restaurant ship and towed to Swansea for the work to be carried out. This work was not undertaken and she was towed to the River Medway and laid up near Strood. *Wingfield Castle* was by now in a sorry condition and it looked as though she would succumb to the local scrapyard. Fortunately Hartlepool Museum was looking for a locally built ship and in 1986 she was bought by the museum and towed back to her birthplace for restoration.

TECHNICAL DETAILS. Identical to the *Tattershall Castle* (page 4). Departing from New Holland in October 1971. Collection of Barry J. Eagles.

LINCOLN CASTLE
The *Lincoln Castle* was launched on the 29th April 1940 by A. & J. Inglis of Glasgow for the London and North Eastern Railway's Hull to New Holland service. The earliest recorded ferry crossing over the River Humber was in 100 A.D. The *Lincoln Castle* was the last ferry built for this service, as the opening of the Humber Suspension Bridge in 1981 ended the ferry operation. *Lincoln Castle* was in fact withdrawn in 1978 after failing a boiler survey. She was sold and became a restaurant on the shore at Hessle until 1986 when, after refitting at Immingham, she was towed to Grimsby to fulfil a similar role.

TECHNICAL DETAILS. Powered by a 3-cylinder triple expansion diagonal steam engine, built by the Ailsa Shipbuilding Company Limited of Troon, producing 850 horse power, with coal fired boilers giving her a speed of 13 knots. Her length is 208 feet 8 inches, with a gross registered tonnage of 598. She carried 12 crew and 1200 passengers.   At New Holland on the 24th September 1976.   Barry J. Eagles.

QUEEN OF THE BROADS
This small steamship was built in 1889 at Cobholm Island and was lengthened in 1896. She was built for excursion work on the Norfolk Broads. In the 1960s she was owned by Pleasure Steamers Limited of Great Yarmouth, who had a fleet of five small steamships. *Queen of the Broads* was the smallest steamship in the fleet and on her withdrawal, her boiler was purchased and refitted in 1978 to the *Puffin*, a 1919 built Admiralty service launch.

TECHNICAL DETAILS. Powered by a compound steam engine of 70 horse power. Her length after lengthening was 70 feet, with a gross registered tonnage of 42. On Breydon Water en route to Oulton Broad on the 3rd August 1971.

YARMOUTH
Another of the Pleasure Steamers fleet was built in 1895 by T. Bradley of Great Yarmouth, for the Great Yarmouth to Gorleston service. She was unusual in being double ended. At the end of the First World War she was used for a short time on the Southampton to Hythe ferry service. She was withdrawn in 1969 and in 1973 bought by Taylor Woodrow for display on the Quay at the St Katherines Dock London.

TECHNICAL DETAILS. Powered by a compound steam engine of 70 horse power, built by Crabtree and Company of Great Yarmouth. Her length is 74 feet, with a gross registered tonnage of 56. She carried 180 passengers. Approaching the Carrow Road Bridge, Norwich in September 1964.

RESOLUTE The *Resolute* was built in 1903 by Edwards and Company Limited of Millwall. This was another double ended steamship built for the Yarmouth to Gorleston ferry service. She was acquired for preservation in 1968 when Pleasure Steamers Limited withdrew her. A new boiler was built for her in 1983 and by 1993 she was still in existence at Shotley.

TECHNICAL DETAILS. Powered by a compound steam engine of 120 horse power, built by Plenty and Co. of Newbury. Her length is 73 feet, with a gross registered tonnage of 71. She carried 316 passengers. At Great Yarmouth on the 21st June 1964.

SOUTHTOWN

This was another small steamship of the Pleasure Steamers Fleet, built in 1896 at Great Yarmouth. She was sold for scrap at the end of 1965 and was towed away and cut up in Holland. The steamships of Pleasure Steamers Limited use to sail from the Town Hall Quay in Great Yarmouth. A typical cruise in the mid-1960s was a two-hour Broadland Cruise for six shillings (thirty pence!). The same amount bought a two-hour harbour cruise. The most expensive cruise was fifteen shillings (seventy-five pence). For this sum of money you departed from Great Yarmouth at 9.30 a.m., and cruised to Wroxham Broad, returning at 6.30 p.m., almost two shillings (ten pence) per hour!

TECHNICAL DETAILS. Powered by a compound steam engine of 150 horse power, built by Crabtree and Company of Great Yarmouth. Her length was 91 feet, with a gross registered tonnage of 72. Moored at Great Yarmouth on the 18th July 1965.

QUEEN OF THE SOUTH
This ship was built in 1931 for the London and North Eastern Railway's River Clyde service, as the *Jeanie Deans* (page 52) by the Fairfield Ship Building Company of Glasgow. In 1948 she became part of the British Transport Commission's Scottish Region. Three years later she was transferred to the Caledonian Steam Packet Company and was sold at the end of 1965 to the Coastal Steam Packet Company Limited being renamed the *Queen of the South* for operations on the River Thames. Old sailors have always stated that changing a ship's name brings bad luck. In this case it was true as the *Queen of the South* had two disastrous seasons, with breakdowns even after overhaul and being fitted with a bow rudder. Her owners went bankrupt and this fine old paddler was sold for scrapping in Antwerp in October 1967.

TECHNICAL DETAILS. Powered by a 3-cylinder triple expansion steam engine, built by Fairfields of Glasgow, with oil-fired boilers, giving her a speed of 15 knots. Her length was 257 feet 10 inches, with a gross registered tonnage of 839. She had accommodation for 1,480 passengers.

Off Tower Pier on the 28th May 1966.

Previous page: **CONTEST** The steam tug *Contest* was built in 1933 by A. Hall of Aberdeen for T. W. Elliot, for use on the River Thames. She was the second tug of that name for her owners, the previous *Contest* having been built in 1883. The tug firm of Elliots was founded in the 1860s. One of their tugs, *Warrior,* had been one of the first tugs to reach the *Lusitania* after she had been torpedoed and saved 74 lives. Elliots became part of Ship Towage in 1950, eventually being taken over by the Alexander Towing Company in 1975. This company has recently been taken over by Howard Smith Towage. *Contest* was withdrawn in 1972. Her sister, the *Challenge,* is at present preserved at Marchwood opposite Southampton's Western Docks.
TECHNICAL DETAILS. Powered by steam reciprocating engine, producing 1,150 horse power. Her gross registered tonnage was 213.
Passing North Woolwich on the 10th May 1965.

JOHN BENN   The increase in the number of passengers and vehicles wanting to use the Woolwich Ferry caused the *John Benn* and the *Will Crooks,* to be ordered from J. Samuel White of Cowes. They were both delivered in May 1930 and cost £74,000. They were slightly larger than the two previous ferries and used simple condensing engines. These ferries carried a crew of 15 comprising a captain, mate, four deck hands, a deck boy, three engineers, a leading stoker, three stokers and a storekeeper. *John Benn* was sold for scrap in 1963.
TECHNICAL DETAILS. Powered by steam reciprocating engines, driving two paddle wheels, producing 750 horse power. Their length was 166 feet, with a gross registered tonnage of 621. Plying her way across the Thames on the 9th August 1960.

SUECIA

This magnificent turbine steamer was launched at the Wallsend yard of Swan Hunter and Wigham Richardson on the 24th January 1929 for Swedish Lloyd, the sistership of the *Britannia* (page 15). She was built for the Gothenburg to London service. Passengers were landed at Tilbury and the cargo at Millwall Dock. In March 1937 she was sunk by a tanker the *Kollbjorg*. *Suecia* was raised, repaired and back in service just over three months later. She was laid up for the duration of the Second World War, Sweden being a neutral country. She re-entered service after a refit in 1946, followed by a major engine overhaul in 1954. In October 1966 she was sold to the Hellenic Mediterranean Lines of Piraeus and renamed *Isthmia*. Six years later, in 1972, she was sold to Turkish ship breakers in Istanbul, where she was broken up.

TECHNICAL DETAILS. Identical to *Britannia* (page 15).   Passing Gallions Point on the 10th May 1965.

BRITANNIA

The *Britannia* was identical to the *Suecia* (Page 14), but was launched from the Walker yard of Swan Hunter and Wigham Richardson on the 27th February 1929. *Britannia*'s career paralleled that of her sister, being laid up during the Second World War. She was sold along with her sister to the Hellenic Mediterranean Lines in October 1966 and renamed *Cynthia*. For the next seven years she sailed on her new owners route from Marseilles-Genoa-Piraeus-Alexandria-Port Said-Beirut. On the 22nd October 1973 she arrived at Savona in Italy for breaking up.

TECHNICAL DETAILS. Powered by 3 Parsons geared turbines, driving a single screw, producing 5,700 shaft horse power, giving a maximum speed of 19 knots. Their length was 376 feet 4 inches, with a gross registered tonnage of 4,216. Leaving Millwall outer dock on the 24th April 1965.

GLEN STRATHALLAN
The nautical training ship *Glen Strathallan* was built in 1928 by Cochrane and Sons Limited of Selby. She was built as a private yacht for a resident of Douglas on the Isle of Man. *Glen Strathallan* served with the Royal Navy during the Second World War and was returned to her owner at the end of the conflict. The owner died in 1954 and the ship was left to the Shaftesbury Homes. The ship spent the next five years alongside the *Arethusa* on the River Medway. In 1960 she was chartered to the King Edward VII Nautical Training College and spent the next nine years steaming up and down the Rivers Thames and Medway with deck cadets. In 1969 she needed heavy and costly repairs and it was decided that her useful life was over. In accordance with her former owner's wishes, she was scuttled off Plymouth.

TECHNICAL DETAILS. Powered by a steam reciprocating engine. Her gross registered tonnage was 330. Passing North Woolwich on the 24th June 1967.

MEDWAY QUEEN
A veteran of Dunkirk, *Medway Queen* was built in 1924 by the Ailsa Shipbuilding Company Limited of Troon for the New Medway Steam Packet Company. She steamed from Chatham to Southend calling at several Thames estuary piers. Her moment of glory came when she rescued more than 7,000 troops from Dunkirk in the Second World War. She was withdrawn in 1963 and in 1965 was towed to the Isle of Wight where she was used as a restaurant. This venture failed and after laying derelict until 1984 she was towed on board a pontoon to Chatham. After several sinkings, she has found a new berth at Damhead Creek in the Hoo peninsula, where her plucky preservation society is restoring her.

TECHNICAL DETAILS. Powered by a compound diagonal steam engine producing 1,000 horse power giving her a speed of 13 knots. Her length is 179 feet 9 inches, with a gross registered tonnage of 316. She carried 828 passengers. Passing Sun Pier, Chatham on the 31st August 1963.

KINGSWEAR CASTLE
Kingswear Castle was built in 1924 by Philip and Sons of Dartmouth for the River Dart Steamboat Company. Her route was from Dartmouth up the River Dart to Totnes. She remained in the West Country for 41 years until withdrawal in 1965 and was purchased by the Paddle Steamer Preservation Society in 1967. *Kingswear Castle* moved to Rochester in 1971 after being laid up in the Isle of Wight. After being fully restored, she recommenced operations in 1985 and sails during the summer to several destinations from her base at Chatham. She is still coal fired.
TECHNICAL DETAILS. Powered by a compound diagonal engine, built by Cox and Company of Falmouth in 1904, for a previous *Kingswear Castle*, she has a coal fired boiler, and has a speed of 8 knots. Her length is 108 feet with a gross registered tonnage of 94. She carries 235 passengers.
Passing Chatham Dockyard on the 22nd September 1985. Barry J. Eagles.

MAID OF ORLEANS
This beautiful ship was launched on the 17th September 1948 by William Denny and Brothers of Dumbarton for the British Transport Commission. She had been ordered by the Southern Railway Company before the nationalisation of the Railways in 1948. Most of the Southern's ships came from Denny of Dumbarton. During her refit in the winter of 1958/9 she had a "fireman's helmet" extension fitted to her funnel to help keep soot away from her decks. *Maid of Orleans* was the first "Channel Packet" to be fitted with stabilisers. She sailed on the service from Folkestone to Boulogne and Dover to Calais. It was a sad day when she left her lay-up berth at Newhaven on the 6th November 1975, being towed by a Spanish tug, bound for Santander and demolition.

TECHNICAL DETAILS. Powered by 2 Parsons single reduction geared turbines, producing 11,000 shaft horse power, giving a maximum speed of 22 knots. Two Foster Wheeler boilers supplied steam at 280 lb per square inch. Her length was 341 feet, with a gross registered tonnage of 3,776. She carried 1,400 passengers. Departing from Dover on the 15th September 1974. Barry J. Eagles.

SIR WILLIAM WALKER
This steam collier was built in 1954 by Austin and Pickersgill Ltd of Sunderland, one of a quartet built for the Central Electricity Authority (in 1958 this became the Central Electricity Generating Board). They were built to transport coal from the north east coalfields, through the ports of Blyth, Jarrow, Sunderland and Seaham. Their major destination was the Brighton B power station at Shoreham. On occasions *Sir William Walker* brought cargos of coal to power stations at West Thurrock, Tilbury and Kingsnorth. In 1979 it received an extensive refit which gave the ship a further four years of use until withdrawal for breaking up at Manchester in 1983.

TECHNICAL DETAILS. Powered by one three cylinder reheat triple expansion engine built by North Eastern Marine Engineering Company Limited of Sunderland, producing 1,475 horse power. Two oil fired boilers supplied steam at 220 lb per square inch. This gave a speed of 11 knots. Its length was 342 feet, with a gross registered tonnage of 2,901. Approaching Shoreham on the 29th October 1983. Barry J. Eagles.

SIR JOHN SNELL

Sir John Snell was built in 1955 by Hall Russell and Company Limited of Aberdeen for the Central Electricity Authority. This is one of a trio coming from the same builder, the other ships were the *Charles H. Merz* and *James Rowan*. The fourth member was the *Sir William Walker* (page 20). They were all named after executives of the Central Electricity Authority. They were the last steam colliers built for this service. With the advent of nuclear, gas and oil fired power stations, they were redundant by the early eighties and were consigned to the breakers yard. There was an attempt to preserve the *James Rowan*, but this unfortunately failed.

TECHNICAL DETAILS. Powered by one three cylinder reheat triple expansion engine built by North Eastern Marine Engineering Company Limited of Sunderland producing 1,700 horse power. Two oil-fired boilers supplied steam at 220 lbs per square inch, this gave a speed of 11 knots. Their length was 340 feet, with a gross registered tonnage of 2,947.   Approaching the lock at Shoreham on the 7th October 1978. Barry J. Eagles.

Left: **WHIPPINGHAM** This majestic paddle steamer was built in 1930 by the Fairfield Shipbuilding and Engineering Company Limited of Glasgow for the Southern Railway's service from Portsmouth to Ryde and summer excursions. She took part in the evacuation of Dunkirk and on the 1st June 1940 brought 2,700 troops out of the famous French Port. For the rest of the Second World War *Whippingham* became a minesweeper and then an anti-aircraft ship. After war service she was refitted and returned to her former duties. Her sister ship *Southsea* did not survive the war, having been mined off the mouth of the River Tyne on the 16th February 1941. *Whippingham* made her last voyage on the 1st September 1962 and left Portsmouth on the 17th May 1963, being towed to Ghent for scrapping by Van Heygen Freres.

TECHNICAL DETAILS. Powered by a 2 cylinder compound diagonal engine, built by Fairfields, with coal-fired boilers giving her a speed of 16 knots. Her length was 254 feet with a gross registered tonnage of 825. She carried 1,183 passengers. *Whippingham* at Ryde Pier on the 1st September 1962.

Above: Paddlebox of *Whippingham* at Ryde Pier on the 1st September 1962.

SANDOWN
Sandown was launched on the 1st May 1934 at the Dumbarton yard of William Denny and Brothers for the Southern Railway's service from Portsmouth to Ryde. She had a sister the *Ryde* (page 3). She was requisitioned in 1939 for minesweeping duties, being based on the Forth. *Sandown* resumed normal service in early 1945 and made her last crossing on the 19th September 1965. She was sold for breaking up in Belgium a few months later.

TECHNICAL DETAILS. Powered by a 3-cylinder triple expansion diagonal steam engine built by Denny of Dumbarton, with coal-fired boilers giving a speed of 14 knots. Her length was 216 feet with a gross registered tonnage of 684. She carried 1,000 passengers. Passing between Portsmouth and Ryde on 17th July 1960.

VENUS

Venus was built in 1948 by Camper and Nicholsons of Gosport for the Port of Portsmouth Steam Launch and Towing Company. She was built for the Gosport Ferry service and for excursion trips around Portsmouth Harbour. *Venus* led a busy life transporting the dockyard 'mateys' and their bicycles to and from Portsmouth to Gosport. She was the last steam vessel built for her owners. In 1966 she was sold to Blue Funnel Cruises of Southampton, where she cruised from the Royal Pier to various destinations such as up the Hamble and Beaulieu Rivers. In late 1969 she was converted to diesel propulsion. In 1978 *Venus* was sold for cruising on the River Thames from Charing Cross. She is now based in Brisbane as a sailing vessel; her engine is preserved in the Southampton Maritime Museum.

TECHNICAL DETAILS. Powered by a compound steam engine built by Plenty of Newbury of 200 horse power. Her length is 73 feet, with a gross registered tonnage of 74. Departing from Portsmouth on the 17th March 1962.

FERRY PRINCESS
This steam ferry was built in 1948 by Camper and Nicholsons of Gosport for the Gosport and Portsea Waterman's Steam Launch Company. She was built, like her contemporary the *Venus* (page 25), for the Gosport ferry service. In 1961 *Ferry Princess*'s owners amalgamated with the owners of *Venus* to form the Portsmouth Harbour Ferry Company. In 1967 *Ferry Princess* was sold to Thames Pleasure Craft Limited and converted to diesel for operation on the River Thames from Westminster to Tower Pier and Greenwich.

TECHNICAL DETAILS. Powered by a triple expansion steam engine of 200 horse power. Her length is 73 feet, with a gross registered tonnage of 79.
Awaiting a berth at Portsmouth on the 17th March 1962.

CALSHOT
The tug tender *Calshot* was built in 1930 by John L. Thornycroft of Southampton for the Southampton, Isle of Wight and South of England Royal Mail Steam Packet Company Limited, otherwise known as Red Funnel. She was built for tug and towage work and also for tendering liners anchored in the Cowes roads which avoided the additional time and cost of docking in Southampton. *Calshot* was replaced in 1964 with a new diesel tug tender also named *Calshot*. The older *Calshot* was sold to a subsidiary of the Holland America Line. Converted to diesel she was renamed *Galway Bay*, and tendered liners in the Republic of Eire. She also undertook excursions to the Irish Aran Islands. In 1986 she became surplus to requirements and was bought by Southampton Museums. She arrived in Southampton on the 10th October 1986 and is currently moored in Southampton Docks.

TECHNICAL DETAILS (AS BUILT). Powered by a pair of triple expansion steam engines, with an indicated horse power of 1,500 her length is 147 feet with a gross registered tonnage of 679. In Southampton Docks on the 3rd September 1961. Collection of Barry J. Eagles.

ISLE OF SARK
The turbine steamer the *Isle of Sark* was launched on the 12th November 1931 by William Denny and Brothers of Dumbarton for the Southern Railway. She was one of a trio of sister ships, her sisters being the *Isle of Jersey*, and the *Isle of Guernsey*. She was built with a Maierform bow. She and her sisters were built for the Channel Island service. She made the last sailing on the 28th June 1940 from the Channel Islands before the German occupation. *Isle of Sark* served on several routes and on various duties during the Second World War. She made her first crossing on her old route after the ending of hostilities on the 24th June 1946. She was withdrawn from service on the 29th October 1960 with her final destination at Ghent, where she arrived for breaking up on the 7th April 1961.

TECHNICAL DETAILS. Powered by 4 Denny geared turbines driving twin screws producing 5,400 horse power, giving a speed of 19 knots. Her length was 306 feet, with a gross registered tonnage of 2,233. She carried 1,400 passengers in two classes.

In Southampton Water, August 1960. Collection of Barry J. Eagles.

NORMANNIA

The second ship of that name was launched on the 19th July 1951 by William Denny and Brothers of Dumbarton for the British Railways Board. She was built for the Southampton to Le Havre route with her maiden voyage commencing from Southampton on the 3rd March 1952. *Normannia* plied this route for the next eleven years and was then sent to Hawthorn Leslie on the Tyne for conversion into a stern loading drive on car ferry. After her major refit she was transferred to the Dover to Boulogne service and made her first voyage in her new role from Dover on the 21st April 1964. She worked several other routes, such as the Weymouth to the Channel Islands, until withdrawal. On the 29th November 1978 *Normannia* departed from Newhaven under her own steam bound for Spain and breaking up.

TECHNICAL DETAILS (AS BUILT). Powered by 2 Denny geared turbines driving twin screws, producing 8,000 shaft horse power, giving a speed of 20 knots. Her length was 309 feet, with a gross registered tonnage of 2,217. She carried 1,400 passengers in two classes.

Approaching Weymouth on the 1st April 1978. Barry J. Eagles.

FALAISE

The *Falaise* was the last turbine steamer to be delivered to the Southern Railway. She was launched on the 25th October 1946 by William Denny and Brothers of Dumbarton. She was built for the Southampton to St Malo service and her maiden voyage commenced from Southampton on the 14th July 1947. On the 1st January 1948 she became part of the British Railways fleet. *Falaise* was sent to Vickers Armstrong's Tyne yard on the 4th January 1964 for conversion into a car ferry and returned to service on the Newhaven to Dieppe route on the 1st June 1964. *Falaise* remained on this route for nearly nine years, before being transferred to the Weymouth to Channel Islands service. She remained on this service from October 1973 until the 21st August 1974, when she sailed for laying up in Holyhead. On the 24th December 1974, she departed from Holyhead under tow for breaking up in Spain.

TECHNICAL DETAILS (AS BUILT). Powered by 4 Denny single reduction geared turbines driving twin screws, producing 8,500 shaft horse power, giving a speed of 20 knots. Her length was 310 feet 6 inches, with a gross registered tonnage of 3,710. She carried 1,527 passengers in two classes. Berthed at Weymouth on the 30th June 1974. Barry J. Eagles.

MAID OF KENT
Known as the Pocket Liner the *Maid of Kent* was launched on the 27th November 1958 by William Denny of Dumbarton for the British Railways Board. She was built for the Dover to Boulogne car ferry service. Her maiden voyage on this route commenced on the 28th May 1959. *Maid of Kent* remained on this service until 1974, when she transferred to the summer only Weymouth to Cherbourg service. She made a few calls to Guernsey, as well as serving on the Stranraer to Larne and the Holyhead to Dun Laoghaire routes for a short time. 1981 was to be her last season and she was sent to Newhaven for laying up. On the 6th April 1982 she left Newhaven under tow, bound for Spain and breaking up.

TECHNICAL DETAILS. Powered by 2 Denny double reduction geared turbines driving twin screws, producing 11,500 shaft horse power, giving a speed of 20 knots. Her length was 373 feet, with a gross registered tonnage of 3,920. She carried 1,000 passengers in one class and 190 cars. Backing out of Weymouth on the 2nd October 1980. Barry J. Eagles.

CAESAREA
The third ship of that name was launched on the 29th January 1960 by J. Samuel White and Company Limited of Cowes for the British Railways Board. *Caesarea*, the Roman name for Jersey, and her sister *Sarnia* (Page 63), were the last passenger ships built specially for the Channel Islands service. *Caesarea*'s maiden voyage commenced on the 3rd December 1960. With the advent of the car carrying ferries to the Channel Islands, *Caesarea* became surplus to requirements and she made her last sailing to Weymouth on the 6th October 1975. She was transferred to the Dover station, where with the exception of a months return to the Channel Islands in 1978, she remained. On the 7th October 1980 she arrived at Newhaven for laying up. *Caesarea* was sold to the Superluck Enterprise Company of Hong Kong on the 20th December 1980. She was renamed *Aesarea* and she had been bought for conversion into a gaming ship and floating hotel. She sailed for Hong Kong, but no conversion work was carried out on her and after a six year lay up she was broken up in South Korea.

TECHNICAL DETAILS. Powered by J. Samuel White double reduction geared turbines driving twin screws, producing 8,500 shaft horse power giving a speed of 20 knots. Her length was 322 feet with a gross registered tonnage of 4,174. She carried 1,400 passengers in one class. Arriving at St. Peter Port, Guernsey on the 28th April 1978. Barry J. Eagles.

CALEDONIAN PRINCESS
Affectionately known as the 'Caley P.', this turbine steamer was launched on the 5th April 1961 by William Denny and Brothers of Dumbarton for the Caledonian Steam Packet Company. She was built for the Stranraer to Larne service and her maiden voyage commenced on the 16th December 1961. *Caley P.* remained on this route until July 1968, when she began to lead a nomadic existence. She was eventually transferred to the Weymouth to Channel Islands service in August 1974 to replace the *Falaise* (page 30). With a few exceptions she remained on this service until the 16th July 1981 when she made her final sailing from the Channel Islands. She made a few sailings from Dover and then she was sent to Newhaven for laying up. In December 1982 she was sold to the Quadirini group and renamed the *Tuxedo Princess*. She was converted into a recreation centre and in this role she has been berthed at Gateshead and other locations.

TECHNICAL DETAILS. Powered by 2 Denny double reduction geared turbines driving twin screws, producing 11,500 shaft horse power, giving a speed of 20 knots. Her length is 353 feet with a gross registered tonnage of 3,630. She carried 1,400 passengers in two classes and 156 cars. Arriving at St. Peter Port, Guernsey on the 4th February 1981. Barry J. Eagles.

PRINCESS ELIZABETH
This popular paddle steamer was built in 1927 by Day Summers of Southampton for Red Funnel Steamers. She was built for the Southampton to Cowes ferry service and summer excursion work. Her foredeck was kept clear so that she could carry ten cars. She was called up in the Second World War and after taking part in the Dunkirk evacuation she became a minesweeper. Returning in 1947, she was given a complete refit and converted to oil firing. For the next twelve years she resumed her former duties until being sold for further service. She operated out of Torquay and Weymouth for the next few years, until sold in 1967. Her boiler and engines were removed and since then has led a nomadic existence, being at Langstone, River Thames, River Seine before ending up as a museum ship at Dunkirk.

TECHNICAL DETAILS (AS BUILT). Powered by a compound diagonal steam engine built by Day Summers of Southampton, giving her a speed of 14 knots. Her length is 195 feet, with a gross registered tonnage 371. She carried 700 passengers and 10 cars.

Approaching Weymouth on the 7th June 1965.

EMBASSY

This paddle steamer was built as the *Duchess of Norfolk* in 1911 by D. & W. Henderson of Glasgow. She was built for the London and South Western and the London Brighton and South Coast Railway's joint fleet for the Portsmouth to Ryde service. *Duchess of Norfolk* was called up for service as a minesweeper in the Mediterranean in the First World War. She then returned to her normal route and in 1923 became part of the Southern Railway fleet. In 1937 she was sold to Cosens of Weymouth, refitted and renamed *Embassy*. She was called up again for minesweeping duties in the Second World War and was returned to Cosens in 1947 for refitting and conversion to oil firing. *Embassy* gave her owners another 20 years of service until she was sold for breaking up in Amsterdam in 1967. She had a sister the *Duchess of Richmond*, which sank after striking a mine on the 28th June 1919.

TECHNICAL DETAILS. Powered by a compound diagonal steam engine, giving her a speed of 14 knots. Her length was 190 feet, with a gross registered tonnage of 381. Approaching Swanage on the 2nd August 1964.

CONSUL This veteran paddle steamer was built as the *Duke of Devonshire* in 1896 by R. & H. Green Limited of London. It was built for the Devon Steamship Company and was used mainly on summer excursions, from such ports as Exmouth and Torquay. Used as a minesweeper in the First World War, serving in the Dardanelles, it returned to its old haunts until being sold in 1933. After several changes of ownership, it was eventually bought by Cosens of Weymouth in 1938 and renamed *Consul*. *Consul* remained with Cosens on the South Coast until 1963 when it was sold and renamed the *Duke of Devonshire*, operating from Hastings and Eastbourne. This venture failed and after lay-up on the River Dart it arrived at Southampton for breaking up in October 1968.

TECHNICAL DETAILS. Powered by a compound diagonal steam engine, built by J. Penn and Son of Greenwich. Length was 167 feet, with a gross registered tonnage of 257. Approaching Weymouth Pier on the 16th May 1964.

ROEBUCK
Roebuck was launched on the 24th March 1925 by Swan Hunter and Wigham Richardson Limited on the Tyneside for the Great Western Railway. *Roebuck* and her sister *Sambur,* were built for the service from Weymouth to the Channel Islands. They would carry livestock and 600 tons of general cargo. There was also accommodation for six passengers. During the Second World War they were used as barrage balloon vessels and afterwards went back to Weymouth to resume the Channel Island service. *Roebuck* made her last sailing to Weymouth on the 27th February 1965. She was bought for demolition by Lacmots Limited of Queensborough, but she was resold to a Belgian firm for breaking up. *Sambur* was withdrawn in March 1964 and broken up in Holland.

TECHNICAL DETAILS. Powered by a pair of triple expansion steam engines, driving twin screws, giving a speed of 12 knots. Her length was 211 feet, with a gross tonnage of 866. Alongside at Weymouth on the 16th May 1964.

ST MAWES
This handsome tug was built in 1951 by H. Robb of Leith for the British India Steam Navigation Company. She was originally named *Arusha* and was built for service in far Eastern ports. She carried a large crew of four officers and eleven men. In 1955 she was bought by the Falmouth Towage Company and four years later her name was changed to *St Mawes*. She was kept busy for the next couple of decades, manoeuvring ships in and out of Falmouth. In the 1970s she was equipped for oil dispersal work, which took her further afield. With the dramatic rise in the cost of fuel oil and with her large crew, she became uneconomical and *St Mawes* was withdrawn for breaking up.

TECHNICAL DETAILS. Powered by a triple expansion steam engine, producing 800 horse power.

Departing from St Peter Port in the Channel Islands on the 20th March 1978. Barry J. Eagles.

BRISTOL QUEEN

This elegant paddle steamer was launched on the 4th April 1946 by Charles Hill and Sons of Bristol for P. & A. Campbell. She was built for excursion work in the Bristol Channel making runs from Bristol to Weston, Ilfracombe and the Island of Lundy. *Bristol Queen* went to Cosens of Weymouth for a major overhaul during the winter of 1962/3. This gave her an extended lease of life. She was, however, soon withdrawn and after a proposal to use her as a museum in Bristol failed, she was broken up in Belgium in 1968.

TECHNICAL DETAILS. Powered by a 3-cylinder triple expansion diagonal steam engine built by Rankin and Blackmore of Greenock, producing 2,700 indicated horse power giving a speed of 18 knots. Her length was 244 feet 7 inches, with a gross registered tonnage of 961.

Backing away from Ilfracombe, August 1960. Collection of Barry J. Eagles

CARDIFF QUEEN
Cardiff Queen was launched on the 26th February 1947 by the Fairfield Shipbuilding and Engineering Company of Glasgow for P. & A. Campbell. She was a scaled down version of *Bristol Queen* (page 39) and was the last paddle steamer to be built for her owners. *Cardiff Queen*'s routes were excursions around the Bristol Channel and from several South Wales ports. She went further afield in 1963 undertaking a three day trip from the Bristol Channel to the Scilly Isles. This proved to be a great success and was repeated the following year. *Cardiff Queen* made her last excursion to the Isle of Lundy on the 21st September 1966 and was then laid up and offered for sale. The only confirmed offer came from Cashmores of Newport, where she was broken up in 1968.

TECHNICAL DETAILS. Powered by a 3-cylinder triple expansion diagonal steam engine, built by Fairchilds of Glasgow, producing 2,200 indicated horse power, giving her a speed of 17½ knots. Her length was 240 feet with a gross registered tonnage of 765. Approaching Weston-Super-Mare on the 30th May 1964.

LADY OF MANN
This perfect turbine steamer was launched on the 4th March 1930 by Vickers Armstrong of Barrow-in-Furness for the Isle of Man Steam Packet Company. She was built in the centenary year of her owners and was known as the centenary ship. At 3,104 gross tonnage she was the largest ship ever built for the company. She was called up for war service and had a very active war, being at Dunkirk in 1940. She managed to evacuate 4,262 men, right up to D-Day, when she was used as a headquarter ship. In 1946 she was overhauled by Cammell Laird at Birkenhead and resumed her sailings from Liverpool to Douglas. This popular ship remained on this route until August 1971, when she was sold for breaking-up to Arnott Young of Glasgow.

TECHNICAL DETAILS. Powered by 2 sets of single reduction geared turbines, producing 11,500 shaft horse power, driving twin screws, giving her a speed of 23 knots. Her length was 360 feet with a gross registered tonnage of 3,104. She carried 81 crew and 2,873 passengers. Approaching Douglas on the 30th August 1969.

BEN-MY-CHREE (IV).
The first ship built as an oil burner for the Steam Packet was launched on the 5th April 1927 by Cammell Laird of Birkenhead. It was also the first ship built for the company after the First World War, at a cost of £200,000. *Ben-My-Chree* (IV) was at Dunkirk, where the ship rescued 4,095 troops. The *Ben*, as she was affectionately known, had a busy war and was a headquarters ship off Omaha Beach on D-Day. *Ben-My-Chree* IV returned to her owners during June 1946 after an extensive overhaul. The Steam Packet used the *Ben* for another 19 years before she was sold for breaking-up in Belgium in December 1965.

TECHNICAL DETAILS. Powered by 2 sets of Parsons single reduction geared turbines, producing 10,300 shaft horse power, driving twin screws, giving a speed of 20½ knots. Length was 355 feet, with a gross registered tonnage of 2,586. Carried 82 crew and 2,586 passengers. Approaching Douglas on the 25th July 1963.

KING ORRY (IV).
The first of the Steam Packet's war replacement vessels was launched on the 22nd November 1945 by Cammell Laird of Birkenhead. This vessel replaced its predecessor which was lost at Dunkirk on the 30th May 1940. It was the fourth ship of this name and served its owners until its withdrawal on the 30th August 1975. *King Orry* was bought for demolition at Bury, but on the 2nd January 1976 it broke away from its berth in a storm and ran aground. Refloated and resold, *King Orry* was finally broken up at Rochester, Kent in 1979. One of its boilers, starboard turbines and a propeller, are in the National Maritime Museum collection.

TECHNICAL DETAILS. Powered by 2 sets of Parsons single reduction geared turbines, producing 8,500 shaft horse power, driving twin screws, giving a speed of 21 knots. Its length was 325 feet, with a gross registered tonnage of 2,485. It carried 68 crew and 2,163 passengers. At berth at Douglas on the 24th July 1963.

TYNWALD **(V).** Named after the ancient parliament of the Isle of Man, *Tynwald* (V) was launched on the 25th March 1947 by Cammell Laird of Birkenhead. She replaced her predecessor, which was sunk by enemy action at Bougie, 150 miles east of Algiers, on the 12th November 1942. She cost £461,859 to build and gave her owners good service until her withdrawal in August 1974. She had only one blot on an exemplary career, when she sunk the barge *Eleanor* on the River Mersey on the 25th February 1952. She was sold to Cashmores of Newport who resold her to a Spanish firm, who broke her up at Avtles in February 1975.

TECHNICAL DETAILS. Identical to *King Orry* (IV) (page 43), except gross registered tonnage was 2,493. Approaching Douglas on the 9th August 1973.

MONA'S ISLE (V) was the fifth post-war ship for the Steam Packet Company and was launched on the 12th October 1950 by Cammell Laird
of Birkenhead. She was the last of the company's fleet to use low pressure turbines. She cost £570,000 to build and entered service during March 1951. On the
8th June 1955 she sank a fishing vessel the *Ludo*, causing the death of one of the *Ludo*'s crew. *Mona's Isle* (V) went aground off Peel on the 15th February 1964
and had to be towed to Birkenhead for repairs. Her end came on the 30th October 1980 when she left the River Mersey for breaking-up.
TECHNICAL DETAILS. Similar to *King Orry* (IV) (page 43), except gross registered tonnage was 2,495, and carried 67 crew and 2,268 passengers.
Approaching Douglas on the 29th August 1979. Barry J. Eagles.

SNAEFELL **(V).** Named after the Isle of Man's highest mountain, *Snaefell* (V) was launched on the 11th March 1948 by Cammell Laird of Birkenhead. With their classic lines, black and white hull and red and black funnels, The Isle of Man Steam Packet's immaculate ships were known to the Liverpudlians as "Mini Cunarders". *Snaefell* (V) cost £504,448 to build and had an efficient and quiet career. Sold for scrap, she was towed to Blyth during November 1978.
TECHNICAL DETAILS. Identical to *King Orry* (IV) (page 43), except gross registered tonnage was 2,489. Backing out of Douglas on the 9th August 1971.

MANXMAN (II).

MANXMAN (II). This splendid ship was the last "classic" ship built for the Steam Packet Company. *Manxman* (II) was launched on the 8th February 1955 by Cammell Laird of Birkenhead. It cost £847,000, a substantial increase from its predecessor. *Manxman* (II) had different engines from the other five post-war ships built for the company. Apart from a few minor collisions the vessel led a successful and uneventful life. *Manxman* (II) was the last operational traditional steamer in the British Isles and it was a sad day when it made its last sailing to Douglas, on the 4th September 1982. On the 3rd October 1982 it sailed to Preston to take up a static role. This was unsuccessful and it is surprising after many mishaps, the ship is still in existence.

TECHNICAL DETAILS. Powered by 2 sets of Pametrada double reduction geared turbines, using superheated steam at 350 lbs per square inch. This produced 8,500 shaft horse power, driving twin screws, giving a speed of 21 knots. Its length was 325 feet, with a gross registered tonnage of 2,495. It carried 68 crew and 2,393 passengers. Approaching Douglas on the 27th August 1979. Barry J. Eagles.

MANX MAID (II).

This ship was the first car ferry built for the Steam Packet and was launched on the 23rd January 1962 by Cammell Laird of Birkenhead. She loaded cars from the side by a spiral set of ramps. *Manx Maid* (II) cost £1,087,000 to build and was the first vessel in the company to be fitted with stabilisers. Her maiden voyage from Liverpool was on the 23rd May 1962. In 1979 she was fitted with a bow thruster to help her manoeuvring. The steep rise in the cost of heavy bunker oil hastened her demise and on the 9th September 1984 she was withdrawn. After several attempts to preserve her failed, she was sold for breaking-up.

TECHNICAL DETAILS. Powered by two sets of Pametrada double reduction geared turbines, using superheated steam at 350 lbs per square inch. This produced 9,500 shaft horse power, driving twin screws, giving a speed of 21 knots. Her length was 325 feet, with a gross registered tonnage of 2,724. She carried 60 crew, 1,400 passengers and 90 cars. Backing out from Douglas on the 15th July 1979. Barry J. Eagles.

BEN-MY-CHREE (V).
The last steam turbine vessel built for the Steam Packet was launched on the 10th December 1965 by Cammell Laird of Birkenhead. The cost was £1,400,000 and as well as being the 14th vessel built for the Isle of Man Steam Packet by Cammell Laird since 1910, she was also the last. She made her maiden voyage on the 12th May 1966. A steam powered bow thruster was fitted to her in 1978, as well as the triple bell steam whistle from the *Tynwald* (V) (page 44). She was withdrawn on the 17th September 1984. Several attempts made to sell her for further service failed and she was towed away for breaking-up in August 1989.

TECHNICAL DETAILS. Identical to *Manx Maid* (II) (page 48), except gross registered tonnage was 2,724.
At Liverpool landing stage on the 26th August 1979. Barry J. Eagles.

CONISTER

The *Conister* was destined for a long life and was launched on the 13th September 1921 by Browns Shipbuilding and Dry Dock Company Limited of Hull. She was built for Cheviot Coasters Limited of Newcastle Upon Tyne as the *Abingdon*. In January 1932 she was bought by the Isle of Man Steam Packet Company for £5,500, and her name changed to *Conister*. She went about her humble duties serving her owners well for the next 33 years, until 1965, when she was sold to Arnott Young of Glasgow for breaking-up. *Conister* was the last coal burning ship in the company's fleet.

TECHNICAL DETAILS. Powered by a triple expansion steam engine built by C. & D. Holmes of Hull, producing 430 brake horse power, giving her a speed of 10 knots. Her length was 145 feet with a gross registered tonnage of 411. Moored at Douglas on the 25th July 1963.

JEANIE DEANS
This graceful paddle steamer was launched on the 7th April 1931 by the Fairfield Shipbuilding and Engineering Company of Glasgow, for the London and North Eastern Railway Clyde River service. Her maiden voyage was to Arrochar on the 8th May 1931 and became very popular as the crack ship of the River Clyde. Called up for war service, she became a minesweeper and then an anti-aircraft ship. Released from war service in 1945, she resumed her service on the River Clyde. *Jeanie Deans* was transferred to the Caledonian Steam Packet on the 5th November 1951. She served her new owners for another 13 years and made her last sailing on the 28th September 1964. She was sold to the Coastal Steam Packet Company Limited for cruising on the River Thames being renamed *Queen of the South* (page 11). Her success turned into a disaster.

TECHNICAL DETAILS. Powered by a 3-cylinder triple expansion steam engine, built by Fairfields of Glasgow, with oil-fired boilers, giving her a speed of 18 knots. Her length was 257 feet 10 inches, with a gross registered tonnage of 839. She had accommodation for 1,480 passengers.

Approaching Gourock on the 22nd August 1964.

Previous page: Departing from Dunoon on the 20th August 1964.

WAVERLEY The preserved paddle steamer *Waverley* was launched on the 2nd October 1946 by A. & J. Inglis Limited of Pointhouse for the London and North Eastern Railway's River Clyde service. She replaced a 1899 built paddle steamer of the same name that was sunk at Dunkirk. She operated on services and excursions from Craigendoran. On the 5th November 1951 she was transferred to the Caledonian Steam Packet. *Waverley* was withdrawn from service in 1973 and sold for £1 to the Paddle Steamer Preservation Society for active preservation. She has gone from strength to strength, venturing around the whole coast of the British Isles. *Waverley* has just completed a major refit with finance from the Heritage Lottery Fund.

TECHNICAL DETAILS. Powered by a 3-cylinder triple expansion steam engine, built by Rankin and Blackmore of Greenock, with oil-fired boilers, giving her a speed of 15 knots. Her length is 239 feet 11 inches, with a gross registered tonnage of 693. She has accommodation for 1,350 passengers.

Approaching Dunoon on the 19th August 1964.

KING GEORGE V
This popular turbine steamer was built in 1926 by William Denny and Brothers of Dumbarton for Turbine Steamers Limited. It was built for the service from Greenock to Campbeltown and Inveraray. On the 3rd October 1935, *KGV* as it became known, was taken over by David Macbrayne Limited and placed on cruising to Iona and Staffa from Oban. *KGV* was called up for war service and took part in the evacuation from Dunkirk. After the vessel was demobilised it went back to Macbraynes and returned to its pre-war service. *KGV* continued on this service until withdrawal in 1974. It was bought for conversion into a restaurant, but unfortunately caught fire and was broken up in South Wales.

TECHNICAL DETAILS. Powered by 6 Parsons single reduction geared turbines, producing 3,500 shaft horse power, giving a speed of 21 knots. Length was 260 feet 6 inches, with a gross registered tonnage of 985. It had accommodation for 2,000 passengers.   Arriving at Oban on the 7th July 1971.

QUEEN MARY II
This turbine steamer was built in 1933 by William Denny and Brothers of Dumbarton for Williamson Buchanan Steamers Limited. She cost her owners £61,805 to build and was used on services to Arran. Her name was changed from *Queen Mary* to *Queen Mary II*, due to Cunard wanting to use her name for their new ocean liner. This was accomplished by Williamson Buchanan adding the suffix II to their steamer's name. She was acquired by the Caledonian Steam Packet Company in 1943. *Queen Mary II* had an uneventful, but successful, life and in 1957 had a major overhaul, being converted to oil-burning, losing one funnel in the process. She was withdrawn from service in 1979 and was sold to Glasgow Council for use as a museum. This deal fell through and eventually she was resold for use as a restaurant on the Thames replacing the *Caledonia* (page 56). She now looks splendid with her reinstated twin funnels.

TECHNICAL DETAILS. Powered by 3 direct drive Parsons steam turbines, built by Denny of Dumbarton, with coal-fired boilers, later replaced by oil-burning ones. This gave her a speed of 19 knots. Her length is 263 feet 4 inches, with a gross registered tonnage of 1,014. She had accommodation for 1,820 passengers.

CALEDONIA
The paddle steamer *Caledonia* was launched on the 1st February 1934 by William Denny and Brothers of Dumbarton for the Caledonian Steam Packet Company service from Gourock, Wemyss Bay and Largs. She was requisitioned as a minesweeper in the Second World War and renamed *H.M.S. Goatfell*. In 1942 she was converted to an anti-aircraft ship and shot down two enemy aircraft. *Caledonia* had an extensive refit after the war by her builders and re-entered service on the 20th May 1946. She was converted to oil-burning during her 1954/55 winter overhaul. Withdrawn from service in 1969, she was bought by Bass Charrington for service as a restaurant on the River Thames. On the 7th April 1980 she caught fire and was so badly damaged she had to be broken up. Her engine is preserved at the Hollycombe Steam Museum in Hampshire where it is occasionally steamed.

TECHNICAL DETAILS. Powered by a 3-cylinder triple expansion steam engine, built by Denny of Dumbarton, with coal-fired boilers later replaced by oil-fired ones. This gave her a speed of 14 knots. Her length was 230 feet, with a gross registered tonnage of 623. She had accommodation for 1,730 passengers. Approaching Dunoon on the 23rd June 1968.

DUCHESS OF HAMILTON
The turbine steamer *Duchess of Hamilton* was built in 1932 by Harland and Wolff Limited of Govan for the Caledonian Steam Packet. She was used on the same routes as her running mate, *Duchess of Montrose* (page 58). During the Second World War she was used on trooping from Stranraer to Larne. After a refit in 1946 she resumed her normal duties. A further refit in 1956 resulted in her being converted to oil-burning. *Duchess of Hamilton* was withdrawn in 1972 and laid up in Greenock. She was sold to become a floating restaurant in Glasgow, but was sold two years later for breaking-up.

TECHNICAL DETAILS. Powered by 3 direct drive Parsons steam turbines, built by Harland and Wolff of Belfast, with coal-fired boilers, later replaced by oil-fired ones. This gave her a speed of 19 knots. Her length was 272 feet 3 inches, with a gross registered tonnage of 801. She had accommodation for 1918 passengers. Approaching Largs on the 20th August 1969.

DUCHESS OF MONTROSE
The turbine steamer *Duchess of Montrose* was built in 1930 by William Denny and Brothers of Dumbarton for the Caledonian Steam Packet Company Limited. She was used for long distance excursions from Gourock to Inveraray, Arran via Kyles and Campbeltown. She remained on the River Clyde during the Second World War. In 1956 she had a major overhaul and was converted to oil burning. *Duchess of Montrose* was withdrawn on the 30th August 1964 following a half-day cruise from Gourock and on the 25th September 1965 arrived at Van Heyghen Freres yard at Ghent for breaking-up.

TECHNICAL DETAILS. Powered by 3 direct drive Parsons steam turbines, built by Denny of Dumbarton, with coal-fired boilers, later replaced by oil-burning ones. This gave her a speed of 18 knots. Her length was 273 feet, with a gross registered tonnage of 794. She had accommodation for 1,854 passengers. Approaching Largs on the 21st August 1964.

DALMARNOCK

The beautiful lines of the *Dalmarnock* hide her humble standing as a sewage disposal ship. She was launched on the 8th May 1925 by William Simons and Company Limited of Renfrew for the Corporation of Glasgow. She was built as a sludge disposal ship and cost £48,058 to build. She took her name from the Dalmarnock Sewage Purification Works, from where she took treated sewage for disposal at sea. In 1958 *Dalmarnock* had a major overhaul and was converted to oil-firing, costing £40,000. After 45 years of faithful service she was sold on the 14th January 1971 for breaking-up at Cairnryan.

TECHNICAL DETAILS. Powered by two 3-cylinder triple expansion steam engines, built by W. Simons of Renfrew, driving twin screws, producing 1,200 horse power. Built with coal-fired boilers, later replaced with oil-fired ones. She had a speed of 11 knots. Her length was 260 feet, with a gross registered tonnage of 1,371. She carried 1,400 tons of sewage sludge. Passing Gourock on the 23rd August 1969.

SHIELDHALL

This vessel, the last and most famous sludge steamer, was launched on the 7th July 1955 by Lobnitz and Company Limited of Renfrew for the Corporation of Glasgow. She cost £291,000 to build and took her name from the Shieldhall Sewage Purification Works. She was the second ship of that name, the first *Shieldhall* having been built in 1910 and scrapped in 1955. In March 1977 she was sold to the Southern Water Authority. She was laid up for 2½ years until the 9th June 1980, when she returned to service, carrying sludge from Southampton to a disposal point off the Isle of Wight. Five years later she was withdrawn from service and on the 28th July 1988 was sold to the Solent Steam Packet Limited for active preservation.

TECHNICAL DETAILS. Powered by two 3-cylinder triple expansion steam engines, built by Lobnitz of Renfrew, driving twin screws, producing 1,600 horse power, with two oil-fired boilers. This gives her a speed of 13 knots. Her length is 268 feet, with a gross registered tonnage of 1,792. She carried 1,800 tons of sewage sludge. She now carries 150 passengers. Approaching Gourock on the 23rd August 1969.

MAID OF THE LOCH
This paddle steamer is land locked and strictly not a coastal steamer. She was built in 1952 by A. & J. Inglis of Pointhouse, Glasgow, for the British Transport Commission's Loch Lomond service. In 1957 she was transferred to the Caledonian Steam Packet Company, still continuing her role of providing cruises around the loch. Her construction was unusual in that her funnel and superstructure are of aluminium. *Maid of the Loch* was transported by her builders in sections to Balloch for reassembly. In 1981 she was withdrawn and in spite of many schemes to reactivate her, she is still laid up at Balloch Pier.

TECHNICAL DETAILS. Powered by a 2-cylinder compound diagonal steam engine, built by Rankin and Blackmore of Greenock, with oil-fired boiler, producing 1,050 horse power, giving her a speed of 12 knots. Her length is 208 feet, with a gross registered tonnage of 555. She has accommodation for 1,000 passengers. At Balloch Pier on the 8th July 1969.

SIR WALTER SCOTT

Although not a coastal steamer the *Sir Walter Scott* has many similarities with them. It was built in 1900 by William Denny and Brothers of Dumbarton for the Loch Katrine Steamboat Company for operation on Loch Katrine. Now owned by the Strathclyde Water Department, the vessel makes hourly cruises from Trossachs Pier. Smokeless fuel is used in her new boiler, fitted in 1956, cleanliness being of the utmost importance as Loch Katrine supplies water for the City of Glasgow. This fine old ship is still in operation.

TECHNICAL DETAILS. Powered by a triple expansion steam engine, producing 140 horse power. Length is 110 feet 5 inches, with a gross registered tonnage of 115. It carries 416 passengers. Approaching Stronachlacher Pier on the 15th July 1969.

INDEX

Sarnia is the roman name for Guernsey. She is the sistership of the *Caesarea* (Page 32) and her techicnal details and history are very similar. *Sarnia* in drydock at Southampton in 1962. Barry J. Eagles

BIBLIOGRAPHY

Steamers of British Railways, Clegg & Styring, Stephenson 1962
West Coast Steamers, Duckworth & Langmuir, Stephenson 1966
West Country Passenger Steamers, G. Farr, Stephenson 1967
Railway & Other Steamers, Duckworth & Langmuir, Stephenson 1968
South Coast Pleasure Steamers, Thornton, Stephenson 1969
British Nationalised Shipping, Clegg & Styring, David & Charles 1969
British Paddle Steamers, G. Body, David & Charles 1971
Island Lifeline, C. Chappell, Stephenson 1980
Royal River Highway, F. L. Dix, David & Charles 1985
Steamships of Europe, A. Deayton, Conway 1988

WILL CROOKS The final member of the quartet built by
J. Samuel White of Cowes. In the course of a days work, ten tons of coke
would be used on this vessel. *Will Crooks* followed its brothers to the
scrap yard in 1963 when three new diesel ferries replaced them.
TECHNICAL DETAILS. (See Page 13 *John Benn*)
Plying her way across the Thames on the 9th August 1960.